MARY MOTHER OF GOD

Chris O'Donnell O. Carm.

Mary Mother of God

the columba press

First published in 2012 by
the columba press
55A Spruce Avenue, Stillorgan Industrial Park,
Blackrock, Co. Dublin

Cover by Bill Bolger
Origination by The Columba Press
Printed by Gemini International Limited

ISBN 978 1 85607 797 2

Author's Note

This little volume originally appeared in Czech. It was commissioned to be one of a series of meditative texts all having the same simple format. Each had about forty significant texts with a reflection of some 350 words spread over two pages.

The original text prepared in English was translated into Czech.

Later the same English text was translated into Irish.

Now the reflections are offered in the original English.

Contents

Devotion

The Churches

ONE

Never enough about Mary

The phrase 'never enough about Mary' (*de Maria numquam satis*) has long been ascribed to St Bernard (d. 1153), but it may in fact have originated with St Grignon de Montfort (d. 1716). Though we may sense its truth, the axiom must be used with some care; it is not a universal principle.

We cannot argue that there should always be more dogmas about Mary. The church has come into peaceful certainty of four great truths about her: she is Mother of God, immaculately conceived, ever-virgin and assumed into heaven. It is a more important task for the church to grasp the meaning of these dogmas than to seek to develop others.

It is quite different when we think of her place in the history of salvation. We can never say enough about the wonder and beauty of her role in God's plan; we will never praise God sufficiently for her. When we have said all we can, we will only have begun.

Is our prayer to her always deficient too? Here we need some care. In the spiritual life, quality counts for much more than quantity. Our prayer to Mary will never be sufficient since we cannot capture all of God's love for her, nor express fully the power of her intercession with God. The answer is not necessarily to say more prayers, but to enter into the truths of what we say: one slowly pondered Hail Mary may be of greater worth than many litanies hastily repeated. Moreover, the prayers that we address to her should always be in the framework of the great prayers of the church, especially its liturgy.

'Never enough about Mary' is not an encouragement to exaggeration in doctrine or prayer forms. Its profound truth lies in an invitation to love Mary without limit, to mirror completely her complete dedication to God's will, and to serve her Son with all our hearts.

TWO

'Mary occupies a place in the church,
which is highest after Christ and closest to us.'
(Vatican II, *Church* 54)

It is very hard to speak with accuracy about the sacred mysteries. After all, they are mysteries. It is so easy to distort God's wonders. This magnificent quotation from Vatican II gives a very sure guide to thinking about Mary, the Mother of God.

In the past people liked to exalt Mary, to dwell on her privileges, to heap up praises and devotions. The danger was that they could make Mary remote, almost withdrawing her from the realm of the genuinely human. In the past few decades another approach became common, which was to emphasise what Mary shared with all of us, and in so doing to play down her exceptional graces. Neither approach in itself is healthy or helpful. It may be easier to stay with one or other truth about her. But in this simplification, we deform God's truth. Mary is indeed unique; she is greater than we could possibly imagine. But she is not divine; her place is firmly with creatures.

This text of Vatican II unashamedly proclaims Mary's greatness: she is highest after Christ, but in the church. She is Mother of the Church, she is its matchless beauty, and she is a peerless model. Her greatness, however, does not separate her from us. She is close to us in her humanity. She too walked the way of faith and of suffering. She knows what it is to be human. But she is close to us in another sense. It is God's will to give us to her as her children; as Mother, then, she is involved with all our cares.

We can keep faith with the truths about Mary by avoiding an exclusive emphasis. At one time we can consider her greatness and glory; at another time we can think of her as being very human and close to us. This alternation will be sufficient to protect us from deformation in our devotional life. But maybe we should not be content to rest with alternating approaches, being careful, for example, to correct each statement about glory with one about humanity. We can possibly do better by trying to hold together the two truths: it is the one who is closest to Christ who is at the very same time closest to us.

THREE

The very name of the Mother of God
contains the whole mystery of the plan of the incarnation.
(St John Damascene, d. c.749)

The mystery of the incarnation proved very difficult to formulate accurately. We can easily enough give its elements. Jesus Christ is fully God and fully man. Some people had made mistakes about his divinity: they spoke in a way that would not take in the fact that he was fully God, the Second Person of the Most Blessed Trinity. Others had problems with his humanity: they did not like the idea of the all-holy God having a body. Even when these truths are safeguarded, there is a further problem that can be answered only by saying: he is one, not two.

We can see that these theological ideas could be very difficult matters for ordinary priests, monks and laity; indeed many of them got it wrong. The Council of Ephesus (AD 431) found a solution in a single Greek word, *Theotokos*, which means 'God-bearer'. Now if Mary is really Mother of God, then her Son is truly human; if she is truly Mother of God, then her Son is divine. Moreover, Mary had one Son, Jesus Christ. Therefore we are only speaking of one person, who has to be the divine Person. Very precise: one word solves it all. The churches of the East especially kept using this one word, *Theotokos*, like a litmus test. If anything strange was said about Jesus, they asked how the statement might be squared with Mary being Mother of God.

People can get tired of abstract talk. They can say, 'Does it really matter?' In the case of Mary being Mother of God, it could not matter more. Our salvation depends on Jesus Christ being truly man and truly God, in other words on Mary being Mother of God.

She is not of course Mother of the Divinity. God as Father, Son and Holy Spirit is eternal, and Mary was born in time, somewhat over 2000 years ago. God does not come from her, but God the Son came to her as her Son through the overshadowing of the Holy Spirit.

FOUR

Our All-holy, immaculate, most blessed and glorified Lady, Mother of God and Ever-Virgin Mary
(Byzantine Liturgy)

The churches of the East use frequently in their liturgy the phrase 'Our All-holy, immaculate, most blessed and glorified Lady, Mother of God and Ever-Virgin Mary.' It is her full title in their worship. The title celebrates God's gifts to Mary; no element of it really refers to what Mary did, but rather what she received.

Holiness belongs properly to God alone. Any holiness we may have is from God, made possible by him who shared divine life with us. The Eastern churches speak of divinisation where Western Christians might speak of grace. Mary is in their eyes the most perfectly divinised one. She is therefore, 'All Holy'; she is gifted above all others. She is immaculate, that is, without sin. In the liturgy we pray, 'in your mercy keep us free from sin' (prayer at Mass after the Our Father). So Mary is the one who has most perfectly received God's mercy.

She is 'most blessed and glorious'. We can bless Mary and give her glory, but blessing is fundamentally what God does. When God blesses us, we are given some gift by him. Glory is something that belongs to God. He will allow his favoured one to share in his glory. But above all God has shared something of his beauty and life with Mary.

The East loves to repeat the word *Theotokos* (God-bearer). That is, for them, Mary's greatest glory, to be Mother of God. It is joined with 'Ever-Virgin' so that we are brought more deeply into the mystery of God's plan: mother and virgin.

The churches of the East do not have as much theological speculation as the Catholic Church in the West. They are more concerned with recognising with joy her place in the liturgy and thus in the church. In this liturgy they see her as the most beloved and blessed of all persons; the one who has received most from God.

FIVE

The One who is mighty has done great things for me;
holy is his name.
(*Luke 1:49*)

Mary's song of praise, the *Magnificat*, is a celebration of what God has done for his people and for Mary herself. At the time of the visitation (*Luke 1:39–56*), Mary did not know fully the great things the Lord had done for her, and that he would do in the future. Indeed it was only with Pentecost, and perhaps more accurately, with her death that she learned the full beauty and wonder of God's grace in her.

We talk about the four Marian dogmas, the important truths that the church professes about the Mother of Jesus. Mary is immaculately conceived, Mother of God, ever-virgin and assumed into heaven. They are all mysteries of God's grace. In each of them Mary *receives* rather than *does* something.

From the first moment of her being as a person, she was preserved free from sin. Thus even before she could do anything, God had already poured out his Holy Spirit on her to make her full in holiness. She did nothing to bring this about; it was sheer grace. She became the Mother of God; this was through the Holy Spirit who overshadowed her (see *Luke 1:35*). She is ever-virgin; this again is a grace of the Spirit. She was brought wholly as a person, that is body and soul, to heaven. Again, this is sheer gift.

So we see that what makes Mary splendid and glorious is not so much what she did, but 'the great things' God did for her. In this she is the model for all the disciples of her Son. What will make us in turn holy is God's gift to us. Like Mary we have to accept this gift, we have to believe and to cooperate, but the great deeds are God's, not ours. Hence with her we give thanks as we say about all the good things we have received: 'Holy is his name.'

SIX

*The Blessed Virgin Mary was, from the first moment of her
conception, by the singular grace and privilege of
almighty God and in view of the foreseen merits of
Christ Jesus the Saviour of the human race,
preserved immune from all stain of original sin.*
(Pius IX, 1854)

There can be some confusion about the meaning of this doctrine. Some people confuse it with the conception of Jesus in the womb of Mary by the power of the Holy Spirit. The Immaculate Conception is the conception of Mary. 'Immaculate.' This is a negative word, meaning, 'not spotted or stained'. The stain involved is original sin. The doctrine can be stated simply: 'Whatever original sin is, Mary never had it.' Original sin means that all are born in a state of lacking grace and salvation; grace, in other words, is not inherited. Mary, from the very first moment of her existence, was the most beloved of God and enjoyed grace, which made her holy, sharing in the life of the Trinity.

The Eastern Orthodox and other churches do not celebrate this feast. However, they do have a major celebration of the Presentation of Mary on 21 November, which makes more or less the same point that Mary always fully belonged to God.

In the preface for the Mass we find two themes interwoven. It relates Mary to her Son: it would have been completely inappropriate for the Mother of the Second Person of the Trinity ever to have been under the reign of sin. The preface also points to Mary's relationship to the church, to us. She is God's sign of favour to the church. The perfection of God's plan is already visible in Mary; we wait for God's salvation to clothe us perfectly too.

The feast is therefore a celebration of what God has done for Mary because she was destined to be the Mother of God; it also celebrates what God has done for the church by giving it Mary as advocate and model of holiness; it looks forward to the perfect holiness and beauty that God will eventually give the church.

SEVEN

Mary was a virgin before, during, and after the birth of her Son.
(See Lateran Council I, 649)

The lapidary statement that Mary was a virgin before, during and after the birth of Christ is found in substance at the Lateran Council of 649. This council was anxious to show that the two wills of Jesus, divine and human, were perfectly at one. This was demonstrated by showing that no contamination could have come to Jesus by way of his birth which was from a virgin. Long before this regional council, the church had proclaimed in the liturgy and in the Fathers that Mary was ever-virgin (in Greek *Aeiparthenos*). The first serious objection came from the fourth-century heretic Helvidius whose ideas were quickly quashed by St Jerome (d. 420). It remained in quiet possession until the Reformation.

We know from the New Testament that Jesus was conceived of a virgin and the Holy Spirit (see *Mt 1:20–25; Lk 1:31–35* and creeds). The statement that Mary was a virgin during the birth of Christ does not necessarily demand that we believe in a miraculous birth at Bethlehem. The New Testament texts about the 'brothers and sisters' of the Lord were seldom interpreted during the first 1500 years of Christianity in the sense that Mary had other children.

Two contrary ideas are in circulation today. One is that Mary's perpetual virginity is in some sense a downgrading of marriage. One would answer that the incarnation is such a unique event that our human wisdom about marriage is not very relevant. Again, we have to see that for Mary to be ever-virgin Joseph would have had to acquiesce; one could ask if Joseph would wish to have had conjugal relations with a woman who had conceived by the Holy Spirit? What sense of awe and reverence might he not have had? Love has many expressions apart from sexual intercourse.

Another idea that one hears is a questioning of whether it matters or not that Mary was ever-virgin. This is not a good theological question; theology seeks to understand what God has done or revealed, not to judge whether the divine will is wise or not.

The Virgin Mary has combined perfect human love for Joseph her husband with an undivided love for her Son Jesus and for the mystery who is God.

EIGHT

We proclaim, declare and define as a dogma revealed by God: the Immaculate Mother of God, Mary ever-Virgin, when the course of her earthly life was finished, was taken up body and soul into the glory of heaven.
(Pius XII, 1950, see *Catechism of the Catholic Church*, 966)

The assumption feast came to Rome no later than the sixth century. Since then, it has been found in the Catholic and Orthodox churches. Its main focus is Mary's death or sleeping in the Lord, her birthday into glory. As always we should seek the meaning of a feast in the Preface of the Mass. In it we see that God willed that her body would not be corrupted. Secondly, the assumption is a sign of hope for us who still live on earth.

> You would not allow decay to touch her body, for she had given birth to your Son, the Lord of all life in the glory of the incarnation. Today the Virgin Mother of God was taken up into heaven to be the beginning and pattern of the church in its perfection, and a sign of hope and comfort for your people on their pilgrim way.

Pope Pius XII, in defining the dogma (1950) of the assumption spoke of Mary, said 'body and soul'. Today we might prefer to say: 'Mary fully as a person is glorified.'

The assumption is a model for our future glorification and teaches a proper attitude to our bodies. We look beyond death, which appears to dismantle our personality, to a deeper transformation through the divinisation of grace (see *2 Pet 1:4*). We are not to worship our bodies in vanity; our true beauty is not cosmetic but a work of God. Neither must we despise our bodies, which are in the image and likeness of God (see *Gen 1:27*). We may not all look like fashion models, but there is a profound beauty even in the most broken, diseased or damaged body. So the feast of the assumption, along with that of the transfiguration (8 August), encourages us to have a healthy attitude to our whole being, which is destined for glory.

Once again looking at Mary helps us to appreciate properly our own humanity and destiny. As Mary is now, we are to be.

NINE

The Blessed Virgin is invoked in the church under the titles of Advocate, Helper, Benefactress and Mediatrix
(Vatican II, *Church Lumen Gentium* 62)

The Second Vatican Council (1962–65) had a very difficult debate about the Blessed Virgin Mary. The Council was not divided by the person of Mary herself, but by different views of how she should be presented in the Council documents. One critical question was whether she should be treated in a special document or within the constitution on the church. By the narrowest vote of the whole council (1114 / 1074), it was decided to place the main document of the Council within the church constitution. As she is mentioned in eleven of the sixteen documents of the Council, one cannot claim that the council neglected her.

A second issue that underlined the debates was whether there should be a definition about Mary's mediation. Only a minority of the Council fathers (382) thought that it was opportune to define that she was Mediatrix. The majority pointed especially to two issues: the ecumenical difficulties that would emerge if there were a definition; and the lack of clarity about what exactly the mediation of Mary means.

The council was at pains to point out that stating her to be Advocate, Helper, Benefactress and Mediatrix 'was to be understood in such a way that it neither takes anything away from, nor adds anything to the dignity and efficacy of Christ the one Mediator (*Lumen Gentium* 62; see *1 Tim 2:4*).

These four titles might be said to express in other language two truths: that Mary is our spiritual mother who cares for us; that she is inseparably linked with her Son's saving work (Vatican II, *Liturgy Sacrosanctum Concilium*, 103).

If we contemplate together two statements we can obtain some intuition about what Mediatrix means: on the Cross, Jesus is doing everything for our salvation; at Calvary, Mary is not doing nothing. She shares in his saving work, but does not add to it. She is most concerned that we obtain the fruits of redemption.

TEN

In union with the whole church we honour Mary the Virgin Mother of Jesus Christ our Lord and God.
(Roman Catholic Mass)

Mary is always recalled in the Eucharist of the Eastern and Western churches. In the churches of the East there are the striking icons of the *Theotokos*, the Mother of God, as visual reminders. She is remembered explicitly in the Eucharistic Prayer or *anaphora*.

The church looking up to Mary learns in doing so the essentials of the sacred liturgy. The Mass celebrates in mystery the sacrifice of Calvary. But the centre of the Mass is in heaven; there Jesus Christ is the eternal high-priest in constant intercession (see *Heb 7:24–25*). Mary too is at worship in heaven. So we can join our worship with hers and so enter into the sacrifice of her Son.

Mary is also a teacher of the Eucharist. This is not so much by what she said, though her words, 'Do whatever he tells you' at Cana (*John 2:5*) strikingly reflect Jesus' command, 'Do this in memory of me' (*Luke 22:19*). She is above all the one who shows us how we are to celebrate the sacred liturgy. Mary shows us the right dispositions to bring to the liturgy: total purity of heart, openness to God's word and will, and a complete surrender to God.

Mary was the first tabernacle of the Incarnate Word; she bore him for nine months in eager anticipation, with worship and with longing. Mary was conformed totally to her Son in her love and dispositions. As Teacher of the Spiritual Life (Votive Mass of Roman Rite) she shows us how to offer ourselves in union with her Son, how to receive the gift of divine life, how to show our concern for the whole world in its brokenness and poverty.

In his encyclical on the Eucharist (2003), Pope John Paul II invites us to read Mary's *Magnificat* in a eucharistic key: it celebrates God's plan in its deepest reality, it shows us how we are to celebrate the Eucharist through being humble and open to receive God's faithful love. 'The Eucharist has been given to us so that our life, like that of Mary, may become completely a *Magnificat*' (John Paul II).

ELEVEN

The Blessed Virgin advanced in her pilgrimage of faith,
and faithfully persevered in union with her Son.
(Vatican II, *Church*, 58)

A pilgrimage is a journey to a holy place. The great medieval pilgrimages were to the holy places where Jesus walked: Rome sanctified by the apostles Peter and Paul, and Compostela the shrine of the apostle James. In modern times we have pilgrim places like Lourdes. Mary's pilgrimage took her to two most holy places: Calvary, the site of her Son's sacrifice and death; and the Upper Room, where she and the early church received the Holy Spirit.

Mary's journey was not very far, if we were merely counting kilometres. It is a huge distance psychologically and spiritually. At the annunciation, Mary is told that her Son will be the Messiah King: 'He will be great and will be called the Son of the Most High … The Lord God will give him the throne of his ancestor David … of his kingdom there will be no end' (*Luke 1:32–33*). Mary believes the angel's message. Jesus does not give her any obvious or significant role in his ministry. Other women are mentioned in the gospel as caring for him and the apostles (see *Luke 8:1–3*). Her role was to be that of quiet prayer and hidden support of his mission.

After some thirty years she sees her Son's kingship proclaimed for all to see, but it is in the horror of Calvary: 'Jesus of Nazareth, the King of the Jews' (*John 19:19*). But she remained firm in her lonely faith. Later she knew the joy of the resurrection, but her Son departs again, this time in the ascension. With the others, she awaited the coming of the Holy Spirit. She then vanished again from sight. Her role in the difficult days of the early church was again hidden.

Mary's life of faith is a pilgrimage of constant surprises, of sorrow and of joy. She persevered and remained constant in psychological and spiritual union with Jesus, her Son.

TWELVE

Mary said to the angel, 'How can this be,
since I am a virgin?'
(*Luke 1:34*)

In the annunciation story, the Angel Gabriel has greeted Mary and one specially blessed by God, told her not to be afraid, and outlined from dramatic Old Testament prophecies the destiny of her son: 'great ... Son of the Most high ... Ruler of an everlasting kingdom.' Mary's first recorded comment is the simple question, 'How can this be since I am a virgin?'

The question can be viewed in various ways. It does not necessarily mean that Mary intended remaining a virgin. It would seem more likely that she is asking, 'How?' In other words, what is she to do? She is engaged to Joseph and a virgin, called on by God to be mother of the Messiah. Now what? Where does that leave her engagement to Joseph? From a literary point of view, the question allows Luke to move the account along with the assertion that the Holy Spirit would come upon her and with the sign of the infertile Elizabeth's pregnancy.

Recent commentators have seen here a sturdy and mature response of Mary. She dialogues with the angel and wants assurance and further information about God's plan. She is no vapid figure but a strong woman who is conscious of her duty and position as an engaged woman. Her question has nothing of the derisive unbelief of Zechariah when faced with the same Angel Gabriel six months earlier (see *Luke 1:18–20*).

Tradition has long praised Mary's faith. But it was a genuine human faith that must face questions, can be puzzled, fearful or even anxious. The answer Mary received is the assurance that in turn all of us need and by which we go forward: 'The Holy Spirit will come upon you and the power of the Most High will overshadow you' (*Luke 1:35*). Mary walked in faith and in the power of the Spirit; there is no other path for us except to walk in the darkness of faith. But there will be enough light of faith to allow us to proceed securely and in safety.

THIRTEEN

Then Mary said, 'Here am I, the servant of the Lord;
let it be with me according to your word.'
(*Luke 1:38*)

The second recorded words of Mary are in answer to the Angel Gabriel who has unfolded God's plan to her. She is to be mother of the Messiah through the power of the Holy Spirit. Her response is, firstly, to state her attitude, her self-identity: 'a servant of the Lord'. The Greek word, *doulê*, has more the nuance of 'slave'. She stands before God as fully obedient, claiming no rights.

Mary then utters her acquiescence, often called her *fiat*, from a Latin word, 'Let it be done.' The Greek word is much richer. It does not indicate a passive, acceptance like 'OK, then.' It has the intensity of a desire, 'Oh yes, let it be done.' Mary is not reluctant, but enters fully into God's plan as it has just been revealed to her.

Mary's 'yes' has to be seen in the context of Old Testament faith. Sometimes we think of faith as something just intellectual, about truths that we accept. Biblical faith is this and much more. It involves a submission and acceptance of what God says, what God promises and what God wills. It is a total 'yes' of God's servant. It has an intellectual dimension: the believer accepts as true what God says. It also has the characteristic of trust. The believer knows and is confident that God will really do what he promises. There is also an element of conforming to God's way. Paul speaks of the 'obedience of faith' (*Rom 1:5*).

Mary's 'yes' is her total dedication to God's plan for the world. Theologians like St Bernard (d. 1153) and St Thomas Aquinas (d. 1274) see Mary here also in a representative role. Humanity had sinned. God offers salvation through the Messiah. The world has to accept God's offer of grace and pardon. Mary welcomes salvation on our behalf and is perfectly conformed to the eternal plan.

FOURTEEN

*In the Visitation (31 May) the liturgy recalls the Blessed
Virgin Mary carrying her Son within her, and visiting
Elizabeth to offer charitable assistance
and to proclaim the mercy of God the Saviour.*
(Paul VI, *Marialis cultus*, 1974)

At the Carmelite shrine at Aylesford in England, there is a striking ceramic by the Polish artist, Adam Kossowski (d. 1985). He shows the greeting of Mary and Elizabeth under the shadow of a dove representing the Holy Spirit. The mysteries of Mary are mysteries of the Holy Spirit. In the annunciation, the Holy Spirit overshadowed her. Then Luke, who never adds a careless word, tells us that Mary immediately set out in haste to visit her cousin. Why the haste? She had been given a sign, so she is anxious to see its fulfilment. Her cousin is advanced in pregnancy, and she goes quickly to assist her. These were surely thoughts uppermost in Mary's mind. But God had a wider plan.

Mary greets her cousin, presumably with the customary ordinary word 'peace'. The effects are spectacular. The baby leaps in the womb of Elizabeth; he is sanctified just as the Angel Gabriel had promised his father Zachariah (*Luke 1:15*). Elizabeth is filled with the Holy Spirit and there is a public annunciation of Mary's motherhood of the Messiah. Mary already filled with the Spirit proclaims the saving mercy of God in the *Magnificat*.

Mary who is carrying the Lord greets Elizabeth with the power of the Lord. She is a model for all visits. We too must bring Jesus with us, and greet and serve others in the power of the Lord.

Because Mary is Spirit-filled she can see God's plan for the world. Here she announces God's plan to set the poor free and to pour love on the world. Her proclamation has nothing about ridding the Holy Land of the occupying Romans; she praises God's mercy to her and his faithful love.

The liturgical Feast of the Visitation is largely due to John Jenstein of Prague, Archbishop of Prague (d. 1386), who established it as a feast of intercession for the unity of the church.

FIFTEEN

*The shepherds said, 'Let us now go to Bethlehem
and see this thing that has taken place'*
(*Luke 2:15*)

Theologians write learnedly about the incarnation; lay people
will often look to the Christmas crib. In the crib we see what the
shepherds found, 'Mary and Joseph and the child lying in a
manger' (*Luke 2:16*). They went away 'glorifying and praising
God for all they had heard and seen'.

At Bethlehem God's eternal plan approaches fruition. The
14,000,000 years of our world's history now coming to a climax,
its meaning will, however, only be clear some thirty years later at
Calvary, Easter and Pentecost.

The crib is silent, yes. But if we still ourselves to listen, we will find
that it speaks. It invites us in to savour its mystery. The church's
liturgy points to this mystery:

> In the wonder of the incarnation your Eternal Word has
> brought to the eyes of faith, a new and radiant vision of
> your glory. In him we see our God made visible and so are
> caught up in love of the God we cannot see. (*Christmas
> Preface I*)

There are many instances of God's glory: 'The heavens proclaim
the glory of the Lord' (*Ps 19:1*). The life of tiny insects can fill us
with amazement. But here at Bethlehem is a tiny child, who for
those with faith is a new and radiant vision of this same glory: the
infinite God in the form of a helpless baby. This helplessness is itself an apparition, in which God is seen and speaks to our hearts.
We stand silently before the crib. We cannot work it out. But the
liturgy says, 'We are caught up in love of the God we cannot see.'
We have to allow ourselves to be seized by the mystery of the
Mother and the Child; like Mary we need 'to treasure all these
things and ponder them in our heart' (*Luke 2:19*). Bethlehem is a
place to which we must continually return to ponder its mystery
with the heart of Mary.

SIXTEEN

*When the time came for their purification according to the
Law of Moses, they brought him up to Jerusalem to present
him to the Lord*
(*Luke 2:22*)

Jewish worship at the Temple was both communal, with the people sharing in prayer and song, and also individual. It was also at times very personal, as people approached the priests with offerings for sin, or for intercession.

As described by Luke, the presentation was a complex ceremony. It included the mother's offering for spiritual purification after childbirth. Mary, of course, would not have realised that her virginal parturition left her in no such need. She would have considered herself as an ordinary Jew, bound by the Law of Moses. There was also an offering of the first-born to the Lord, in which Joseph and Mary shared by offering a sacrifice. In their case it was the offering of the poor, two turtledoves or young pigeons. It was a solemn moment as Mary and Joseph consecrated the Messiah to the Lord.

But they did not fully grasp the significance of the event. The Spirit inspired the holy old man Simeon with understanding. He proclaimed Jesus to be 'salvation … a light for revelation to the Gentiles and for glory of the people Israel' (*Luke 2:30–32*). Luke immediately tells us that Mary and Joseph 'were amazed at what was being said about him'. As pious Jews they expected a Messiah for Israel, but here their son was being revealed as a saviour for the Gentiles as well as for Israel. A holy prophetess, Anna then spoke of what he would mean for his people.

Those associated with Mary and Joseph in the infancy gospel of Luke are *anawîm* figures. These were the poor who learned that one could trust only in the Lord. They included Zechariah and Elizabeth, the shepherds, Simeon and Anna, and of course Mary and Joseph. It is these, the poor, who can see into God's plans and proclaim these to others. We see Mary and Joseph learning, from simple people, deeper mysteries about their Son. The poor in spirit and the pure of heart have a hold on the kingdom and see God. (see *Mt 5:3,8*).

SEVENTEEN

The home of Nazareth is the school where we begin to
understand the life of Jesus – the school of the gospel.
(Paul VI, *Address*, 1964)

Nazareth was a small unimportant village, held in some con-
tempt by educated Jews, 'Can anything good come out of
Nazareth?' (*John 1:46*). For some thirty years Jesus, Mary and
Joseph had their home there. The gospels do not tell us much
about their life. Joseph supporting the family by his work as
craftsman; Jesus too learned the trade (*Mark 6:3*).

Devotion to the Holy Family was late in becoming established,
for an intriguing reason. The Western European languages took
over the Latin word *familia*, which meant household or extended
family. Only in the fifteenth century did the word 'family' develop the restricted sense of parents and their own children.
Attention was then drawn to the Holy Family of Nazareth.

We will not enter very much into the truth of Nazareth by looking
at legends created by pious imagination. A key gospel text is the
comment of the inhabitants of the village, when they dismissed
Jesus as having no standing, 'Is not this the carpenter's son? Is not
his mother called Mary?' (*Mt 13:55*). They are saying, 'We know
them, they are insignificant.' This text points to the obscurity of
the life of Jesus, Mary and Joseph.

Beginning with Leo XIII (d. 1903), popes have drawn our attention to the contemplative dimension of what is often called 'the
hidden life' of Jesus, that is, before his public ministry. Our world
needs contemplatives to draw God's blessings on the world and
to deflect the consequences of sin. We have all seen pictures of the
earth from space; the larger cities appear as pinpoints of light.
God looks on the world and sees contemplatives open to his grace
and pleading for the world. They are not only in convents, but
also in houses, in apartments, in the slums surrounding the great
cities of the world, in nomadic Romany camps. Like Joseph, Mary
and Jesus, they are hidden.

Nazareth teaches the true values of humanity. It is the simple, the humble and the pure of heart that most profoundly serve the world; it is indeed only by being simple, humble and pure of heart that we will learn the message of Nazareth.

EIGHTEEN

When the wine gave out, the mother of Jesus said to him,
'They have no wine.'
(*John 2:3*)

The story of the wedding at Cana is one of the best-loved incidents in the gospel. There was a wedding at Cana, about thirteen kilometres from Nazareth. There is a crowd, including Jesus and his uninvited disciples. In the hard subsistence living of the time, a wedding was a great event for relatives, friends, and neighbours. Indeed, when Jesus later tried to teach people about heaven, he often used the image of a wedding feast.

Not having enough wine for the wedding guests was not merely an embarrassment, but a social disaster that would leave the family's name shamed for generations. Indeed lack of wine in the Old Testament was a sign of catastrophe, whereas an abundance of wine was a symbol of God's blessing in all things (see *Isa 24:11* with *25:6*).

We do not of course have a complete account of everything in gospel narratives, much less a video. The evangelist is content to give us the essentials: Mary's words, 'They have no wine.' She obviously expects her Son to do something. His response is not encouraging however we may translate the Greek text. 'Woman, what concern is that to you and to me? My hour has not yet come.' (*John 2:4*) It betrays a reluctance to become involved, implying also that Mary's request was somehow inappropriate.

The gospel here is a skeletal narrative. We do not know what Jesus may have told Mary over the years about his future mission: perhaps that it involved teaching and miracles? Jesus does seem to imply that if the hour had come it would be different.

The address 'Woman' is quite unusual. It is formal, perhaps evoking the first woman Eve. It is solemn, indicating his role as saving Messiah and Mary's role along with him: the concerns of Jesus and Mary will be so much greater than a mere absence of wine.

There is not always an easy or immediate response to prayer. The Syrophoenician woman was apparently teased by Jesus so that she could give full expression to her need and to her faith (see *Mk 7:26–30*). Mary does not see her Son as refusing her and proceeds in faith.

NINETEEN

His mother said to the servants, 'Do whatever he tells you.'
(*John 2:5*)

In the story of the wedding at Cana, we do not have all the information we might like. We cannot know what tone of voice Jesus
used, what look he may have given his mother. We have, however,
the information that the inspired writer wants us to have. He tells
us that Mary said to the servants, 'Do whatever her tells you.'
(*John 2:5*)

The word 'servant' has a lot of rich overtones in the bible. It is the
model for human relationships in the church (see *Mt 20:26*). Mary
can approach the servants. We see later in the text that only the
servants really knew what was going on. They were very compli-
ant. They heard the word of Mary and were then prepared to do a
lot of really hard work. They were asked to fill six large water jars
totalling 550–800 litres (120–180 gallons).

The words of Mary are an echo of a great act of submission of the
Israelites, which we find in various places in the Old Testament:
'All that the Lord has said, we will do.' (*Ex 24:3*) Mary is recalling
the servants and us to obedience to her Son. The changeover from
Old Testament to New is also symbolised by the stone jars for the
Old Law purification now bearing Messianic wine in great abundance. The symbol of displacement of the Old by the New is reit-
erated by the steward of the feast, who proclaims that the New is
better.

Jesus had said to Mary that his hour had not yet come (see *John
2:4*). Yet at her request, the hour was advanced. The evangelist
notes, 'Jesus did this, the first of his signs, in Cana of Galilee, and
revealed his glory, and his disciples believed in him' (*John 2:11*).
Mary as always was instrumental in bringing about the glory of
her Son.

TWENTY

*All these were constantly devoting themselves to prayer,
together with certain women, including Mary
the mother of Jesus, as well as his brothers.*
(*Acts 1:14*)

At the beginning of his second book, Acts of the Apostles, Luke is particularly careful to set the scene for the birth in power of the church at Pentecost. So we have three groups of witnesses assembled: the twelve apostles ('all these', minus, of course Judas), who were witnesses to the public life of Jesus; the women, witnesses to the resurrection; Mary and the brothers, witnesses to the family of Jesus. These are described as being constantly in prayer awaiting the baptism in the Holy Spirit (*Acts 1:5*).

We see Mary at the heart of the infant church. Only she and the Beloved Disciple had remained faithful at Calvary (see *John 19:25–27*). Mary knew from her own experience the coming of the Holy Spirit. She would surely have told the gathered church to be expectant and open to what God would give them. Luke later tells us 'all were filled with the Holy Spirit and began to speak in tongues' (*Acts 2:4*). That 'all' surely includes Mary.

One might wonder if Mary could receive the Holy Spirit again, after the annunciation. We need to be careful about the word 'fill'. We cannot imagine it like a bucket: if it is full, no more can be poured into it. The Holy Spirit comes with love and with gifts and can always give more to those who are open. Indeed members of the Jerusalem church were twice filled with the Holy Spirit (see *Acts 2:4* and *4:31*).

After Pentecost, Mary disappears from the scene. We do not know how long she remained alive. In his encyclical on the Eucharist (*Ecclesia de Eucharistia*, 2003), Pope John Paul II invites us to attend Mass with the mind and heart of Mary, to receive communion whilst mirroring her attitude.

The picture of Mary here is one of her constant prayer for the church, of her complete openness to the Holy Spirit, and of her motherly concern for the church. In this she is not only Queen of the Apostles, that is, of the twelve, but also Queen of all apostles, namely of all those who serve her Son and proclaim his message.

TWENTY-ONE

Mary treasured all these words and treasured them in her heart ...
His mother treasured all these things in her heart.'
(Luke 2:19, 51)

On two occasions we are told by St Luke that Mary took words and events, and treasured them, kept them safe, pondered them in her heart. A somewhat similar idea is that of the prophecy of Simeon that 'a sword will pierce your own soul too' *(Luke 2:35)*. 'Heart' is one of the most primitive human symbols. In the Bible it has a rich range of meanings: we understand with our heart; the heart is the core of our being; it is into our heart that the love of God is poured through the Holy Spirit (see *Rom 5:5*).

Spiritual writers began to reflect on Mary's heart from about the fourth century, beginning perhaps with St Ephrem (d. 373). Since from the Bible we know that the heart can be perverse (see *Jer 17:9–10*) and the source of evil (see *Mark 7:21*), what is stressed in the first millennium is Mary's purity of heart, that is her total surrender to the will of God. By the twelfth and thirteenth centuries devotion to the Heart of Mary was well established, thus coming before devotion to the Sacred Heart of Jesus. But very soon the two hearts of Jesus and Mary were considered together. The classical exposition of the two hearts comes from St John Eudes (d. 1680), who wrote in his book on the Heart of Mary: 'To come to know the Heart of Mary is to come to Jesus; to honour the Heart of Mary is to honour Jesus; to invoke the Heart of Mary is to invoke Jesus.'

St John Eudes celebrated a feast of the Heart of Mary. It was generally celebrated in the Latin church from the time of Pius XII (1942). Now we find it on the day after the feast of the Sacred Heart.

Devotion to the Hearts of Jesus and Mary draws us into the complex visceral relationship of Mary to her Son's work (see Vatican *Directory on Popular Piety and the Liturgy,* 2001, n 174). It invites us to enter into Mary's feelings during her life. In twentieth-century apparitions, the Immaculate Heart stands for Mary herself and her viewpoint on the world. Consecration should lead to our adoption of her attitude in our life.

TWENTY-TWO

More Mother than Queen
(St Thérèse of Lisieux, *Last Conversations*, 21.8.3)

A memorable saying of St Thérèse of Lisieux (d. 1897) was that she would like to be a priest in order just to preach one sermon on the Blessed Virgin.

> I'd first make people understand how little is known by us about her life. We shouldn't say unlikely things or things we don't know anything about ... For a sermon on the Blessed Virgin to please me and do any good, I must see her real life, not her imagined life. I'm sure that her real life was very simple ... We know very well that the Blessed Virgin is Queen of heaven and earth, but she is more Mother than Queen.

Mary was central to Thérèse's life. She began her autobiography by placing it under the guidance of the Virgin, praying in front of the statue of the 'Virgin of the Smile'. Thérèse spoke continually about Mary. She wrote that she redoubled her devotion to Mary after her first confession; she rejoiced to be enrolled as a Child of Mary at fourteen. Her cure through the smile of the Virgin Mary from the strange psychosomatic illness which nearly killed her left an indelible mark on Thérèse's whole life and spirituality.

There would seem to be at least four significant elements in Thérèse's approach to Mary. Mary is the one in whose protection Thérèse feels confident and safe. Secondly, what seems to have impressed Thérèse most about the statue vision was the beauty of Mary smiling on her. Thirdly, Thérèse is firmly drawn to Mary as 'more Mother than Queen'. Thérèse lost her own mother at the age of four and she transferred all her trust to Mary who was her constant companion and confidant. Fourthly, she has a deep passionate love for Mary, even though she had enormous difficulties with the Rosary; she could not understand why the Rosary should be difficult for her who loved Mary so much.

A long poem from her final months, *'Why I love you, O Mary,'* sums up her attitude to Mary. Imitating Thérèse each of us might write a poem or a letter to Mary saying why we love her.

TWENTY-THREE

*Our good Lord showed our Lady to signify the exalted
wisdom and truth which were hers as she contemplated
her Creator ... these filled her with reverent fear and with
humility.*
(Julian of Norwich, d. c.1416)

The Christian tradition is very clear about Mary's virtue of humility. Indeed in the *Magnificat* she refers to her lowliness (*Luke 1:48*; Greek perhaps 'humiliation'). Luke may well have known the Christian hymn, which speaks of the humility of Jesus Christ (see *Phil 2:8*).

Each of us can see why we should be humble: we have all sinned and failed in our Christian journey. But Mary? She was without sin. In the medieval tradition there is a spiritual classic called the *Cloud of Unknowing* that puts before the reader two degrees of humility. The first is what we practice when we look at our sins. This the author calls 'imperfect' humility. Perfect humility, such as Mary had, comes not from looking at ourselves but at God. As she contemplated the infinite beauty of God, she knew her creatureliness. We have the same idea in the text from Julian. Mary was so raised up that her response is reverence and humility.

In our time humility is often misunderstood; many take it as a sign of weakness. Others scoff at 'turning the other cheek' (see *Mt 5:39*) as weakness or timidity; one might, however, suggest that turning the other cheek requires great strength and courage. Another name for humility might be truth. If we know ourselves and see our weakness, then this truth should inform our attitude to ourselves and others, namely humility. If we really appreciate all that God has done for us, that all is gift, then in this truth there is no room for boasting (see *Rom 3:27*).

Mary teaches us to have great joy in God's gifts to us and in us, whilst at the same time turning to him in praise and thanksgiving.

TWENTY-FOUR

*Popular devotion to the Blessed Virgin Mary is an
important and universal ecclesial phenomenon. Its
expressions are multifarious and its motivation very
profound, deriving as it does from the People of God's faith
in, and love for, Christ the Redeemer ... and from an
awareness of the salvific mission that God entrusted to
Mary of Nazareth and Mother of the Lord
and of all humanity.*
(Vatican Directory, *Popular Piety and the Liturgy* [2001] 183)

The word 'popular' can have a specific meaning, which is not
what is well liked or fashionable, but rather what is 'from the people' (see *popolare* etc. in Romance languages). The Latin American
bishops at Medellín spoke of popular devotion as 'a hidden presence of God'. It is the celebration that is incarnated in diverse cult-
ures and in diverse celebration. Catholic theologians avoid the
term 'popular religion' which is sometimes used in a Marxist
sense of what belongs to the people in opposition to institutions
of the church. Popular religiosity has several characteristics. It is
spontaneous, a matter of feeling more than intellectual knowing
or discourse. It is festive rather than focused on effort or reason. It
expresses a radical 'I' who is poor and needy coming to Mary who
is seen as caring and powerful. Popular piety is based on a memory of past gifts and graces. Its origins may be obscure, or lost in
legend, but it is a present reality whose meaning is not necessarily
to be sought in critical history, but in the experience of peoples
over many generations. Many shrines have this feature – sometimes no one knows why people gather in a place, or there can be
different accounts, but what matters is that through prayer and
pilgrimage it has become a holy place.

Taking part in popular piety through pilgrimages, lighting can-
dles, visiting shrines, joining with others in simple prayers can
protect us from pride and an intellectually arrogant faith. It also
fosters the often neglected affective side of religion. Pope Paul VI

wrote: 'Popular piety indicates a certain thirst for God such as only those who are simple and poor in spirit can experience. It can arouse in men and women a capacity for self-dedication … and gives them a keen sensitivity by which they can appreciate the ineffable goodness of God' (*Evangelii nuntiandi,* 1974).

TWENTY-FIVE

Mary, show me your Son; Jesus, show me your Mother
(Prayer ascribed to St Ignatius Loyola, d. 1556)

Devotion to Mary is part of the great heritage of the Catholic and Eastern churches. It takes many forms and expressions. We cannot remain at the level of prayers and exercises. According to Vatican II, true devotion is not a matter of feelings or empty credulity, 'but proceeds from true faith, by which we are led to recognise the excellence of the Mother of God and we are moved to filial love towards our Mother and to the imitation of her virtues.' (*Church Lumen Gentium*, 67)

But there are many excellent Catholics who find devotion to Mary difficult. Sometimes it is from the way Mary was presented to them when they were children. Others, who did not have a good healthy bond with their own human mother, can find devotion to Mary difficult. Such people can feel a sense of guilt from their absence of any warmth or intensity of devotion.

It is for such people that the prayer ascribed to St Ignatius Loyola can be very helpful. Devotion to Mary aims at a relationship. If we can somehow get inside the relationship of Jesus and his Mother, then we would find a genuine devotion that is profoundly enriching.

Mary, show me your Son. It is Mary who above all others knew Jesus. She can draw us into his heart, show us how Jesus loves us and wants us to be his brothers and sisters (see *Heb 2:17*), to be his (see *Jn 15:14–15*), to remain in him (see *Jn 15:5–11*).

Jesus, show me your Mother. Who knows Mary better than Jesus? As a boy and as a man he came to see her beauty, her holiness, and the gifts that his Father had showered on her. He can show us her attitudes, the secrets of her heart; he can show us her tender love and concern for all of us. He can in particular show us how Mary loves him and how she is the beloved daughter of the Trinity. He can show us how we are to be his disciples patterned on his Mother.

This gentle prayer can draw people at any stage of their spiritual journey and can open up great spiritual treasures and graces.

TWENTY-SIX

We fly to thy patronage, O holy Mother of God;
despise not our petitions in our necessities,
but deliver us from all danger,
O ever glorious and blessed Virgin.
(Earliest Marian prayer, third century)

This prayer (*Sub tuum*) is the earliest known prayer to the Virgin Mother of God. It dates from the late third or early fourth century. The first theme is Mary's protection, her patronage. In Roman and into medieval times, people needed a patron, preferably a powerful one, to protect them and look after their interests. In turn they served the patron. It was a two-way relationship.

We fly to Mary; we take refuge in her. It is not an individual prayer, but like the pattern of all prayer, the Our Father, it is a community prayer: we and all the church look for safety in Mary.

Our patron is the holy Mother of God. In the earliest papyrus of the prayer, Mary is called *Theotokos*, a title that would be given to her formally at the Council of Ephesus (431). She is the 'God-bearer,' for her child was truly God. The Mother of God is holy; indeed one of the earliest attributes is 'all-holy'.

We come to Mary in our needs, and we ask her to take our problems seriously. All of us experience dangers that are material and spiritual. We ask Mary to 'deliver us', the same word used in the Our Father (*Mt 6:13 – rydsai*). In the final line we recognise the one to whom we are praying, 'ever glorious and blessed Virgin'. The Second Vatican Council has drawn attention to this ancient prayer (*Church Lumen Gentium*, 66, n 21), and at the same time showed how in the early centuries devotion to her grew 'in veneration and love, invocation and imitation'.

Though we all have troubles, we are encouraged not to keep looking at them. Like the Israelites, we should 'Lift up our eyes to the mountains' (*Ps 121*). They were thinking of Jerusalem, where God dwelt. We, however, raise our gaze to Mary, who brought and still brings God to us. She was a perfect human temple where God truly dwelled. As we contemplate her beauty and glory, our confidence and trust can grow.

TWENTY-SEVEN

Star of sea and ocean,
Gateway to our heaven,
Mother of our maker,
Hear our prayer, O Maiden
(Ninth-century hymn, *Ave maris stella*)

The hymn *Ave maris stella* dates from the ninth century; one hundred years later it is found in the liturgy of the western church. It includes a whole theology of Mary: she is Mother of God, all pure, a caring mother, and our intercessor.

The Marian title, 'Star of the Sea,' is ancient. Even in the time of St Jerome (d. 420) its meaning was not universally clear. Jerome himself seems to have thought that the name 'Mary' itself was most likely to have come from the Syrian *Mar* (a noble lord / lady), and therefore to point to Mary's high state in God's plan.

She is in this hymn 'Star of the Sea,' or in the Litany of Loreto, 'Morning Star'. A star is a minor light; Christ remains the sun. The morning star heralds the dawn that will come with the sun. For thousands of years mariners have used the stars to guide them across the seas.

The symbol of the star is found in the Messianic tradition (see *Num 24:17* – 'a star out of Jacob'). In general stars indicate elevated majesty or grandeur, what is unattainable or out of reach, what is heavenly and shining forth, what is a sign of healing, hope and guidance. Again a star guided the wise men to Bethlehem where they found 'the child with Mary his mother' (*Mt 2:11*).

In Christian tradition, especially the Carmelite school, Mary is seen in another symbol of the sea, where Elijah sees a sign of hope and salvation in the little cloud that rose from the sea to bring life to a barren land (see *1 Kings 18:41–45*).

The great *Akathistos* hymn, the Marian jewel of the eastern churches, hails Mary as 'Mother of the star that never sets' and as 'star causing the Sun to shine,' a dense symbol of the incarnation itself.

Being a symbol, 'Star of the Sea' is open-ended. Different people will pursue its meaning in various ways and depths. It is contemplation more than reasoning that will allow us to penetrate this symbol.

TWENTY-EIGHT

Ave Maria ...

(A favourite prayer of the western Catholic Church)

The most common prayer to Mary in the Catholic Church of the Latin rite begins, 'Hail Mary, full of grace. The Lord is with you.' These are the words of the Angel Gabriel to Mary at the annunciation (*Lk 1:28*). They are a greeting, which gives Mary's identity, 'full of grace'. In the Greek of the New Testament, this has the sense that Mary has received and is receiving the fullness of God's favour. The church's continuing reflection on the scriptures has led it to a grasp of what this favour was. The prayer continues, 'Blessed are you among women and blessed is the fruit of your womb.' These are the words of Mary's cousin at the visitation as she replies to Mary's greeting (*Lk 1:42*). The sense here is praise; indeed it may mean that Mary is truly the greatest of all women.

Though there is much earlier evidence, this part of the prayer became widespread in the western church from the eleventh century and in time became part of the *Little Office of Our Lady*. In the eastern churches we can find variants as early as the sixth or seventh centuries. In medieval Europe the ending, 'Jesus. Amen' is well attested from the fourteenth century. This first part of the prayer was commonly said at morning, noon and evening, when church bells were rung.

The second part of the *Ave*, 'Holy Mary, Mother of God, pray for us sinners, now and at the hour of our death' became more common from the late fifteenth century. The Black Death plague (1348–50) had made people very insecure about death and they turned to Mary's care. The whole prayer became standardised in the Breviary approved by Pope St Pius V (1568).

The *Ave Maria* follows the model of biblical prayer in the psalms and the Our Father. First we praise; then in the light of this thanksgiving or worship, we find confidence to place our requests. The *Ave Maria* does not specify our needs; rather it looks to Mary's constant care, 'pray for us now,' and remembers our supreme hour when we leave this life to go to God. It is thus a prayer of simplicity that reaches up in praise and returns in confidence.

TWENTY-NINE

Salve regina
(Medieval antiphon)

A very popular antiphon or prayer to the Blessed Virgin in the western church is the *Salve regina* (*Hail Holy Queen*). It seems to have first appeared in the eleventh century, and scholars have proposed various authors. Like many prayers to Mary it is in a 'We-style'. It begins with a salutation: 'Hail Holy Queen, Mother of mercy; hail our life, our sweetness and our hope.' These five words (queen, mercy …) sum up medieval attitudes to Mary.

The person or community praying is conscious both of their need and of the power of Mary: 'To you do we cry, poor banished children of Eve. To you do we send up our sighs, mourning and weeping in this valley of tears.' We often think of the Middle Ages in terms of beauty and light, as in the great cathedrals, but they were also dark and pessimistic.

The prayer then turns to the help expected through Mary: 'Turn then most gracious advocate thine eyes of mercy towards us.' Mary takes the place of Eve as mother of the living; Eve was self-seeking, Mary is the advocate.

The centre of the prayer follows: 'And after this our exile show unto us the most blessed fruit of thy womb, Jesus.' The church realises that the Cross exists and cannot be avoided. This prayer puts things into perspective: what is all-important is what happens after death, when we hope that Mary will show us her Son Jesus. The prayer ends by re-echoing its opening, 'O clement, O loving, O sweet Virgin Mary.'

This antiphon became very popular in medieval religious communities and was soon part of the *Liturgy of the Hours*; it was added at the end of Mass by Carmelites and others. Some people may think that its focus is rather narrowly on Mary, even using titles that more properly belong to her Son. If this lovely antiphon were to be our only prayer, or even our only Marian supplication, then it might be unbalanced. But those who say it also use many other prayers, and celebrate the Eucharist and other sacraments. It is thus to be evaluated and treasured within a wider context.

THIRTY

*The Akathistos Hymn, undoubtedly the finest of all Greek
poems in honour of the Blessed Virgin Mary,
remains to this day highly popular throughout the
Orthodox world.*
(Bishop Kallistos of Diokleia)

The greatest Marian hymn of the eastern churches takes its name
from its liturgical setting. It is sung standing (*a-kathistos* – not sit-
ting) on the fifth Saturday of Lent. Many monks use it as a *Little
Office of the Virgin Mary*, and lots of people say it in their homes
before an icon. In some ways it corresponds in the east to the western Rosary.

Scholars still do not agree about its author. It is clear that we meet
here a great poet, an outstanding theologian, a profound contemplative who could synthesise a whole tradition, whilst humbly remaining anonymous. The text comes from the late fifth or early
sixth century.

The *Akathistos* hymn is associated with Mary's help in difficult sit-
uations, traditionally the siege of Constantinople (AD 626). It
opens:

> To thee, our leader in battle and defender, O Mother of God
> We thy servants, delivered from calamity,
> Offer hymns of victory and thanksgiving.
> Since thou art invincible in power,
> Set us free from every peril,
> That we may say to thee, Hail bride without bridegroom.

These last words, 'Hail bride without bridegroom' (Virgin bride)
are a continual refrain throughout the hymn.

The hymn is in two sections. The first twelve stanzas follow the
story of God's appearance in the world as found in the infancy
gospels (*Mt 1–2; Lk 1–2*). It begins in the private world of Mary,
Joseph, Elizabeth and John the Baptist. It then widens out to the
shepherds, Magi and Simeon. The second part (stanzas 13–24)

sings of the mysteries of Mary celebrated in the early church and then her place in the church.

The hymn abounds with symbols taken from the scriptures, the theological and devotional tradition, as well as nature – each one drawing us into deeper wonder at the mystery and wonder of Mary. Any single line could give rise to extended reflection and prayer. The key ideas of the hymn are *Ave*, Virgin, Bride and Alleluia. Like the Rosary, the person and mission of Mary are to be understood in the light of her Son; honouring Mary leads us beyond her to Jesus the Lord.

THIRTY-ONE

*Private revelations do not belong to the deposit of faith. It is
not their role to improve or complete Christ's definitive
revelation, but to help live more fully by it in a certain
period of history.*
(*Catechism of the Catholic Church*, 67)

The words 'private revelations' are a misnomer: they are not 'private' because they are widely diffused; they are not 'revelation' in the strict sense, for this was completed in apostolic times. Private revelations are mostly associated with apparitions, often of the Virgin Mary. There seem to be more of these in recent centuries, but there have been reported appearances of the Virgin from the earliest times of the church, and one can find lists of over a thousand down to the present time, the majority of them being not very credible. Very few apparitions have been approved by church authorities.

Some people say that there are too many apparitions nowadays. Certainly as faith declines, people have become more gullible. But there cannot be too many genuine apparitions. There are many strange reports of apparitions, and we can also find bizarre statements and behaviour in people associated with stories of genuine apparitions. Mary will not lead people astray, but people may easily interpret wrongly or inadequately what the Virgin wished to communicate. Messages are not new revelations; they are mostly concerned with encouraging people to follow the teaching of Christ, often with a specific emphasis on repentance, prayer, penance and moral behaviour.

When church authority, usually the local bishop, investigates a report of apparitions the first concern is accurate information, what actually seems to have happened. Expert opinions are sought from doctors and psychiatrists. Then there is a check for orthodoxy – genuine apparitions will not contradict church teachings. The apparent fruits of apparitions must be good, leading people to Christ, the service of God and others (see *Mt 7:15–20*).

Approval of apparitions generally means the local bishop assert-
ing that there is credible evidence of the supernaturality of the
event and allowing Mass to be celebrated there and possibly the
erection of a church.

A wise approach to apparitions will not chase after apparitions to
the exclusion of the hard Christian imperatives of faith and love. It
will not, however, approach apparitions with a totally negative
mind, declaring them to be impossible. Still prudent caution will
always be preferable to premature enthusiasm.

THIRTY-TWO

The Rosary, though clearly Marian in character, is at heart a
Christocentric prayer. In the sobriety of its elements, it has
all the depth of the gospel message in its entirety, and can be
said to be a compendium of the gospel.
(John Paul II, *Rosarium Virginis Mariae*, 2002)

The Rosary is a favourite Marian prayer of the western church, corresponding in some ways to the *Akathistos* hymn in the east. It gradually arose from the practice of reciting the *Ave Maria* one hundred and fifty times, the number corresponding to the psalms. In the fourteenth century, these were divided into fifteen units of ten *Ave Maria*s. The mysteries, or themes for meditation, developed about the same time. The Rosary in its present form was definitively approved by Pope St Pius V (1569).

The Rosary consists of three main prayers in each unit called a decade: the Our Father, ten *Ave*s and concluding with the Glory be to the Father. But the heart of the Rosary is not these vocal prayers, but the consideration of the salvific events of Christ's life, and their close association with the Virgin Mother. Pope John Paul II noted that 'Without this contemplative dimension, it would lose its meaning,' and he quotes Paul VI as saying, 'Without contemplation, the Rosary is a body without a soul.' Pope John Paul II suggests five powerful ideas: the Rosary is re-membering Christ with Mary, learning Christ with Mary, being conformed to Christ with Mary, praying to Christ with Mary and proclaiming Christ with Mary.

Pope John Paul II has encouraged people to reflect on what the scriptures tell us about each of the mysteries: Joyful in *Luke 1–2*; Sorrowful in the passion narratives of the four gospels, and Glorious mostly in the last chapters of the gospels. In addition he suggested a new set of *Mysteries of Light* for Thursdays: Baptism of Jesus, Cana, Kingdom Preaching, Transfiguration and the Last Supper.

The Rosary is a very simple prayer, but people can find it difficult. It is worth learning to pray it well, since many will find the Rosary a great consolation in sickness and in declining years. Pope John Paul II concluded, 'A prayer so easy and yet so rich truly deserves to be rediscovered by the Christian community.'

THIRTY-THREE

The Angelus, despite the passing of centuries,
retains an unaltered value and an intact freshness.
(Paul VI, *Marialis cultus*, 1974)

From the Middle Ages there has been a custom of reciting the first
part of *Ave Maria* three times when church bells rang at dawn,
midday and evening. It was only with the sixteenth century that
the insertion between the *Aves* of scripture verses about the incarnation became widespread.

'The angel of the Lord declared unto Mary and she conceived by
the Holy Spirit.' This verse recalls the expectation of the Jewish
people, which came to fulfilment at the annunciation. Here we
find the Holy Spirit, whose presence must be continually recalled
if we are to understand the mysteries of Mary's life.

'Behold the handmaid of the Lord. Be it done unto me according
to thy word.' This is the 'Yes' of Mary, spoken on behalf of the
whole human race, which through her welcomes the Redeemer.

'And the Word became flesh and dwelt amongst us.' The scripture texts move from the annunciation scene in *Luke* (*1:26–38*) to
the lapidary statement of *John*, 'The Word became flesh' (*1:14*).
Here we ponder with Mary the central truth of our faith.

A sixteenth-century addition to the Angelus was the medieval
verse, 'Pray for us O holy Mother of God; that we may receive the
promises of Christ.' This shows the eschatological dimension of
genuine Marian prayer, which looks to eternal salvation whilst in-
voking Mary's intercession.

The Angelus ends with either of two similar ancient prayers to the
Father that move forward to the Paschal Mystery of the death and
resurrection of Jesus. It is either the Collect for the feast of the annunciation, or the following: 'Pour forth we beseech you, your
grace into our hearts; that we to whom the mystery of the incarnation was revealed through the message of the angel, may by his
passion and cross be brought to the glory of the resurrection.
Through Christ our Lord. Amen.'

The Angelus succinctly encapsulates the central mysteries of our faith. No wonder that Paul VI could write: 'The Angelus does not need to be revised because of its biblical character ... its rhythm sanctifying the day and its reminder of the Paschal Mystery.'

THIRTY-FOUR

*The Scapular of Our Lady of Mount Carmel is truly
universal and undoubtedly one of the pious practices which
Vatican II described as 'recommended by the
magisterium throughout the centuries'.*
(Vatican Directory, *Popular Piety and the Liturgy* [2001] n 205)

A scapular is part of a religious habit, a wide piece of cloth worn back and front over the shoulders (Latin *scapulae* – shoulder blades) and reaching to the knees or lower. From the Middle Ages lay people sought some association with religious orders, and a common way was to invest them in part of the habit, frequently a reduced scapular. The Brown Scapular of the Carmelite Order has been very popular since the fifteenth century.

The scapular is a symbol, that is a sign that carries a deeper meaning. In a letter to the whole Carmelite Order, the Superiors General, J. Chalmers, and C. Maccise wrote in 2001: 'Reflection on the scapular symbolism implies that we think out and make our own the fact that Mary is our Patroness, who cares for us as Mother and Sister. Our Mother nurtures the divine life within us and teaches us the way to God. Our Sister walks with us in the journey of transformation, inviting us to make ours her own response: "Oh let what you have said be done to me" (*Lk 1:38*). But patronage is a two-way relationship. We receive Mary's care; in turn we are called upon to imitate her and to honour her through fidelity to her Son.'

Wearing of the Brown Scapular is not a quasi-magical totem. It must be a sign of a relationship with Christ along with Mary, one of dependence and love. It will have its fullest meaning only when we are drawn into the contemplation of the divine mysteries. As the symbol of a religious garment, the scapular should also remind us that we are to be clothed with Christ (see *Col 3:10; Rom 13:14*). We may go further and see Mary clothing us with her Son.

For many centuries the Brown Scapular has been seen as a sign of Mary's care and help not only in life's dangers, but also at the time of death and during any purification and healing that a person in purgatory might need.

THIRTY-FIVE

Saturdays stand out among those days dedicated to the Virgin Mary.
(Vatican Directory, *Popular Piety and the Liturgy* [2001] 188)

Since the ninth century, Saturday has been a memorial day of the Blessed Virgin, with a special Mass assigned. We know that in the first century Christians chose Sunday as the Lord's Day. They thus avoided the Jewish Sabbath and commemorated the day of the resurrection. Friday was a day of penance, which recalled the death of the Lord. In some places Saturday was a day commemorating the dead who awaited their resurrection.

The original reason for assignment of Saturday to Mary is not clear, but in reflections over the centuries many grounds have been suggested. 'God blessed the seventh day and made it holy' (*Gen 2:3*); Mary too has been abundantly blessed. The seventh day was the completion of his creation; Mary is God's masterpiece. Saturday prepares for Sunday; Mary prepares us for Christ. When Jesus was in the tomb on Holy Saturday, Mary maintained her faith. On Holy Saturday Mary felt the full pain of the sword that Simeon had said would pierce her heart (See *Lk 2:35*).

Many religious congregations have special observances for Saturdays and in the present liturgy there are several votive Masses for use particularly on Saturdays. In the twentieth century there developed the practice of receiving holy communion on the first Saturday of the month, a practice that clearly parallels the First Friday.

In the Saturday celebrations of the *Liturgy of the Hours* there are many references to Mary. These generally centre around intercession, her help and confident prayer for her care. They also propose imitation of Mary. Such Saturday remembrances serve to develop an awareness of Mary's presence in our lives.

As well as Saturdays, there are Marian months – May (in some southern hemisphere countries November) and October that is traditionally the month of the Rosary. The month of May easily harmonises with the Easter season and its sacraments. The months of October and November can help to recall Mary's role in the communion of saints (All Saints and All Souls, November 1–2). Another prime Marian season is Advent when we look forward to the mystery of Christmas. As Mother of the Church, Mary thus guides us through the liturgical year.

THIRTY-SIX

Help us to live in the truth of the consecration of Christ for the entire human family of the modern world. In entrusting to you, O Mother, the world, all individuals and peoples, we also entrust to you this very consecration of the world, placing it in your motherly heart.
(John Paul II, *Act of Entrustment to Mary*, 25 March 1984)

Since the Fatima apparitions in 1917 there has been renewed interest at every level in the church in consecration to Mary. One could say that the most ancient Marian prayer, *Sub tuum presidium* ('We fly to thy patronage ...') was already an act of entrustment, consecration or commitment.

In recent decades serious theological questions have been raised about consecration. Strictly speaking one can consecrate oneself only to God, for only God has the right to our total dedication and service; in baptism God consecrates us to himself. In the case of Mary it is more than veneration for she is inseparably linked with her Son's saving work (see Vatican II, *Liturgy*, 103); she desires only what her Son desires; she wishes to unite people to him. Dedication to Mary involves dedication to Christ.

There have been several consecrations of the world to Mary by recent popes, for example Pius XII who especially asked for Mary's intercession for peace in the world (1942). In his numerous references to Marian consecration, Pope John Paul II draws on a rich tradition of different expressions which indicate belonging: entrustment, consecration, dedication, recommendation, serving, placing oneself in her hands. He invited the bishops to unite with him in an act of entrustment to Mary on 25 March 1984.

When we speak of Marian consecration, we must think firstly of Mary herself as being the one most consecrated to God. As she is the Mother who intercedes, it is natural that we entrust ourselves to her. As she is exemplar, she forms our response to God in discipleship of her Son. Since she is our Mother, and an abiding presence in our lives, we are right to commit ourselves to her care.

THIRTY-SEVEN

I believe in the communion of saints
(Apostles' Creed)

There are a few words in the Apostles' Creed which we often say without sufficiently attending to their meaning: 'the communion of saints.' Communion (Greek *koinonia*) can be translated as 'fellowship' though this is not a warm word in English; other languages have richer words. Another word that can translate it is 'sharing'.

There is an ambiguity in the phrase for it can mean 'Communion of Holy Persons or of Holy Things.' Some Protestants use the word more for the sharing we have on earth, and the good things like the Bible and sacraments that the Lord provides for us. However, the Roman Catholic and eastern churches more frequently refer to holy persons, often denoting those in glory, those on earth, and later occasionally also those in purgatory. We need to retain both meanings, persons and things.

It is especially the *anaphora* (Eucharistic Prayer) in the east and in the Catholic west that gives a primary experience of the Communion of Saints: the Eucharist is celebrated with the explicit memory of Mary and the saints, with commemoration of the dead, as well as of the living. The celebration of the liturgy in eastern churches has a powerful reminder of the presence of Mary and the saints through the *iconostasis*, or sacred icon screen. These are a visible, almost sacramental reminder of the presence of holy people. The icon is a meeting place between the saint and the believer; it is more important that I allow Mary to look at me through a sacred liturgical icon than that I look at her image.

The communion of saints is both vertical in so far as we join with those in heaven; it is horizontal in the bonds between those on earth who are joined by love in one faith. The Eucharist is celebrated in communion with the Pope and the local bishop.

Two titles given to Mary point to her role in the communion of saints: she is Mother of the Church and she is Queen of Heaven.

THIRTY-EIGHT

*Devotion to the Mother of the Lord is in accord with the
deep desires and aims of the ecumenical movement.*
(Paul VI, *Marialis cultus*, 32)

Mary would at first sight seem to be a stumbling block to ecumenism: there are significant differences between the Catholic Church and the Orthodox as well as the churches of the Reformation in the area of dogma and devotion. There is a place for ecumenism, which must above all be based on truth and be a work of love. In the study of the Virgin across the churches, we find some of the deepest problems facing church unity. In the case of Mary they cannot be avoided and facing them well, serves the ecumenical movement.

Ecumenism is about dialogue, which demands genuine listening to one another in a spirit of mutual respect and learning. Catholics can learn in two ways through ecumenical dialogue about the Virgin Mary. They can find out from other churches new approaches to Mary. In the case of the eastern churches this may be their profound liturgical celebration of her feasts and gifts. From the churches of the reformation, we can learn a deeper biblical spirituality and to bring to Marian devotion good theology as well as the great truths of faith and justification.

There is also a negative learning. Though we may not in the end agree with the positions of the other churches about Mary, we need to listen to their criticisms of our doctrines and devotions. The Orthodox accuse us of excessive theologising about Mary. The Protestant Churches remain extremely sensitive to distortions of faith and of the uniqueness of the mediation of Christ. We will need to look carefully at any prayers or statements that give rise to disquiet among Protestants, especially if they claim Christ or the Holy Spirit are being displaced. Sometimes Catholic positions are misunderstood or poorly expressed. The church is always in need of purification, even in its Marian devotional life.

Looking together at what we can agree about Mary is a service of Christian unity; listening to one another can help us to remove unnecessary barriers. Ecumenism must constantly look to the Spirit who overshadowed Mary and who still hovers over the church.

THIRTY-NINE

There is no 'mariology' in the churches of the reformation, nor any Marian devotion, that is, neither Marian services nor prayer to Mary. On the other hand we can see taking place a renewed reflection on Mary.
(Group des Dombes, *Mary in the Plan of God and in the Communion of Saints*, 1997)

The place of Mary in the churches of the reformation must be expressed with great nuance and clarity. The initial concern of the Reformation was abuses, especially those that were perceived to detract from the centrality of Christ. Mary was not central to its programme. Indeed Luther to the end of his life retained devotion to, and love for Mary.

The scriptures were adopted as the principle and norm for reform. Later this became set as scripture alone, along with Christ alone and faith alone. As the Reformation progressed there was a gradual restriction to what was in the scripture, and a consequent rejection of much post-New Testament development in doctrine and structures. There was too an elimination of devotions, many of which were perceived as non-scriptural and deviant.

During and after the Reformation, positions hardened. Luther was constant in his teaching about Mary's virginity, her divine maternity and the fact that since Christ is our Brother, she is in some way our Mother. In the following centuries, Protestants became ever more negative about mariology, especially the new definitions of the Immaculate Conception and Assumption. Some Lutheran and Anglican Churches still retain the christological feasts that have a Marian dimension, Presentation of the Lord, Annunciation and Visitation.

In recent years some Protestant theologians have resituated the Mother of God in the mystery of salvation and see her as humble servant, admirable witness to the faith and as the foremost of redeemed creatures. Whilst they admire her praise-filled *Magnificat*, direct prayer to Mary is generally rejected. One can

notice a difference between churches, which have assigned scripture readings throughout the year, and churches in which the
choice of the readings is left to the presiding minister. In the latter,
congregations may go for a very long time without being intro-
duced to the scriptural picture of Mary, which is so necessary for
ecumenical progress.

FORTY

In celebrating this annual cycle of the mysteries of Christ,
holy church honours the Blessed Mary, Mother of God,
with a special love. She is inseparably linked with
her son's saving work. In her the church
admires and exalts the most excellent fruit of redemption,
and joyfully contemplates, as in a faultless image,
that which she herself desires and hopes wholly to be.
(Vatican II, *Liturgy Sacrosanctum Concilium*, 103)

The main teaching of the Second Vatican Council (1962–65) is to be found in the eighth chapter of the *Constitution on the Church (Lumen gentium)*. But the text in the *Constitution on the Liturgy (Sacrosanctum concilium)*, promulgated a year earlier, has a density and also a serenity that predated the robust debate in the following session (1964) on how Mary was to be presented. It presents a profound mariology in five points.

It is in celebrating the mysteries of Christ that the church honours Mary. Mary is never alone; she is to be found with her Son and never apart from him.

The church has a special love for Mary. The many titles all draw the believer into praise, wonder and a relationship with a Mother, a Queen, a Sister …

Mary is inseparably linked with her Son's saving work. This simple sentence can drive away conflict about her role. Other titles, which have their own truth, such a Mediatrix, Coredemptorix, might be said to express no more than this simple sentence of the council.

The church sees in Mary the most excellent fruit of redemption. Mary is redeemed; indeed she of all people is the perfectly redeemed. The response of the church to this is admiration and exaltation. The spiritual beauty of the Virgin cannot be possessed or imprisoned; the proper response is wonder and praise.

The church joyfully contemplates, as in a faultless image, what its members are striving for. The vision of Mary is a grace, a blessing, a cause for pleasure and delight. Mary is a mirror of what God's blessings are for all of us.

In a darkened world the vision of Mary is our consolation. It raises our minds to wonder and beauty. It aligns us along God's plan for her and for ourselves. Mary provides moments of refreshment and hope on life's pilgrimage.